women in this town

New York, Paris, Melbourne, Tokyo, Madrid, London

Giuseppe Santamaria

women in this town

New York, Paris, Melbourne, Tokyo, Madrid, London

hardie grant books

To my mom, super woman.

TOWNS

women in this town

I've always had an infatuation with street photography, especially as a record of fashion and the way that ordinary people used to dress and go about their lives.

When I'm shooting for my street-style blog *womeninthistown.com*, I'm always looking for someone who exudes confidence. An individual who dresses for themselves and doesn't care what others think.

This book is snapshot of how women in some of the world's most stylish cities are expressing themselves through fashion in the middle of this decade.

Giuseppe Santamaria

New York

Mod

NOTES

An unassuming look from a distance, this is elevated by the jewellery details on her hands, and in her nose and ears.

Rainbow bright

Jamie Beck
in New York

I met Jamie Beck in 2011, when I had the
opportunity to attend New York Fashion Week
with Tumblr. Her photography and sense of
style are of another time – yet she strikes a fine
balance in keeping her look contemporary. An
old soul who's always looking forward.

On her personal style

I like simplicity and I like quality, which is something that I couldn't really afford before. I always look for timeless, classic pieces. Whenever I can, I like to support designers that I believe in what they're doing and how they make their clothes.

That's more important to me now and that's changed a lot. Obviously, what I wore when I was in college – the colours and the hemlines, all that stuff – that just doesn't feel age-appropriate anymore. I've become more serious about what I do, and about my work, and what I put out there in an image sense. Now with social media I'm very aware of the image that I put out there because a lot of young aspiring female photographers look up to me and I want to be a good role model. I want to show that I respect myself and I can still be feminine. Even though I do a very masculine job, I don't have to give up personal style to go to work. But I have fun with men's fashion. I'll wear brogues when I work and men's button-up shirts and things like that. I steal a lot of my husband's clothes.

On her fashion influences

My grandmother who lived on the East Coast, she was a painter. She always wore these really beautiful blazers and loafers and white purply cropped pants. She was very East Coast and I just loved it. She always wore a blazer with all these necklaces with [fish] hanging on them and stuff. She had really good style and she had really big lashes which, when I was little, I saw that as the most glamorous thing in the world.

Oh, you know, I love photographer Amy Lee Woods, and I think she has amazing style and it's, like, a very unique style. She's one of my icons.

Princess Diana. I used to try to dress like Princess Diana. I had two-piece matching suits and I even had the haircut. Like, the whole thing. Her and Jackie Kennedy.

It was, like, I would just bounce back and forth between the two. Their style's really influenced by love of fashion.

On New Yorker style
Black! I love, love, love riding in a cab, going up Sixth Avenue from here and just looking at all the black. I just feel like it's a stamp of New Yorkers. I like that women are very – it's, like, very powerful – I like that women here are just very, like a jet-ink line of black. It's like, boom, to the point, direct. Get it done. Business time, you know.

But you see that's my window into New York, because obviously you have amazing street-style people who wear crazy, incredible, pieces of, like, art, you know, and colourful clothes like that. But the kind of world in which I swim around is very serious.

On what keeps her in New York
This is where all my work is, the kind of work that I want, that I can only get in New York. I love the work. I love this city. Whenever I come back to New York from someplace else, I have the emotional love in my chest when I see the skyline. I just, I love it. There's always something to do. There's always some new place to discover. You discover things about yourself. There's just a million inspirations everywhere you look, and all your fantasies can play out here, you know. If you want to go listen to Woody Allen play jazz at the Carlyle, or if you want to go to a speakeasy or go bowling, you can do it, and pretty much any time of day. You can go, be like, 'I want a hotdog', and you can have one, and, there's just, I like that overstimulation, and I like the idea that I can spend my entire life here and still learn and see something new, so ...

On the other hand, I do fantasise about how nice it'd be to live in, like, a small town and, like, have a community and have a garden and, you know, wake up in pink and not wake up in a panic. (Chuckles.)

Crop

I love to see people have fun with fashion, especially when they know how to strike a balance. Here, a classic look is brightened by a feathered phone case.

Canadian tux

Rouge

Perhaps a more forgiving way of sporting a tattoo? Spotted in Soho, with her little dog, too.

Paris

Paris grey

Cool blues

NOTES

Just by the quality and structure of her suit, you can tell she's worn some pretty timeless pieces in her life.

SALADES SUR MESURE
TARTES SALÉES
FAIT MAISON

PARADIS

Cuffed

Louise Brody in Paris

Born in London, raised in Pittsburgh and settled in Paris, Louise Brody now lives with her husband in an atelier formally occupided by Picasso. And that is where we met. Louise's well-travelled life and love of books led her to become a freelance graphic designer, creating books for the likes of Suzy Menkes and other fashion elite.

On her personal style

I love dresses. I think it makes a clean line. Also, it's easy because you have just one piece instead of having to think: 'Oh, do those trousers go with that top? Or this skirt, etc.' So for the last few years I have to admit I've been dressing mostly in dresses. Also, to me it's very feminine. I mean, I'm very active and I do a lot of things, but somehow I still feel more comfortable in a dress. I think I've probably got that from my mother, but, it's just the way I feel comfortable. Just a simple black dress or something that I can then dress up. I like fashion jewellery, you know, not real – I have a few real pieces – so long as it's not too over the top and fairly simple.

When I look back, I was very Laura Ashley and flowers when I was, you know, in my 20s, and then I got a bit more sophisticated, I hope!

On her fashion influences

My mother. My mother had a huge amount of style. I could show you some photos. She was beautiful and very, very stylish, and I was the first daughter and she loved dressing me when I was a child and, well, apparently from the age of three I had very clear ideas of how I wanted to dress. I would choose my party dresses and my shoes! So I've always been very conscious of that.

But I also learned a lot from magazines. I mean, I always bought *Vogue* and *Marie Claire* and *Elle*, which I have to admit I do much less frequently today because you can find everything on the internet, and for somebody who really believes in print, I know it's a terrible thing to say!

On Parisan style

Well, French women have so much chic and style. I mean, when I first came here, I was 'the English rose', the girl wearing flowery dresses and long flowing hair.

The French women on the other hand, it was much more the little suits and straight trousers and short hair. I even cut my hair to try fit in! And that definitely influenced me, that way of just always looking chic, even if they're wearing jeans or they're tired, French women always have a way of looking elegant and smart, and it's a way they carry themselves and a way – it's just their attitude. I think they're – I find that English women often are always a bit apologetic about the way they look, whereas French women are much more sure of themselves. It's different again from Italian style, but I've definitely learnt a lot about fashion and style from living in Paris, just watching women and observing people. When I had more time I used to, with a girlfriend, we used to sit in the Café de Flore when it was nice outside with a drink and we'd watch the women go by saying: 'Hmm, five; no, two!' We had a lot of fun.

Somehow the French woman knows how to balance. I've never really seen a French woman overdressed. It's usually more understated than over the top, and I think that's very important.

On what keeps her in Paris
Visually, you never tire of Paris. I mean, I've been here for 25 years and I can still walk across one of the bridges and have my breath taken away because the architecture is just, it's so wonderful. You can walk most places, which of course is the best way to get the feel of a city. There are so many cafés where you can watch people or be watched, and it's also a wonderful visual influence in the city itself. All the time it's feeding my mind and my ideas, and for me that's vital because it, you know, inspires the work that I do, and so I feel very, very, very lucky to live here, and also to live in a space like this which is, you know, daily inspiration.

Under plaid

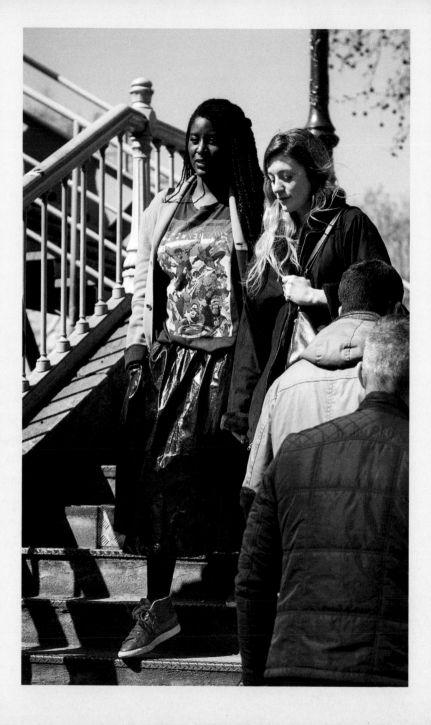

NOTES

Canal Saint-Martin, my favourite spot in Paris to photograph the young and carefree inhabitants of the neighbourhood.

Bowler

NOTES

With the first signs of spring also comes the first signs of bare skin.

TOWN

Melbourne

Brim and ribbon

Christmas in Australia;
bold prints and earthy
colours are a sign of the
holidays.

Lace dots

Summer air

Hayley Hughes in Melbourne

One of Australia's original fashion bloggers, Hayley Hughes' bold style (and personality to match) have always been on my radar. Now working as a stylist in her home town, her Japanese-inspired looks have started a movement in the Melbourne fashion scene.

On her personal style

I've definitely always loved fashion. I played with my Barbie dolls and made their outfits as a child, and then I would go to op-shops (thrift stores) and create looks and cut up and sew things. And then, as a teenager I was really into this look that was called grunge and I would wear, like, crazy flares and tie-dyed dresses over the top and have blue hair and piercings, and then I went to art school and I was obsessed with the '80s and I would wear legwarmers and crazy '80s things. I've just always been obsessed with expressing myself through fashion, so my style has definitely evolved over the years, but it's always been kind of out there and quirky, for sure.

On her fashion influences

I don't know where my interests in fashion came from because my mum and my grandma aren't very interested in fashion, really, but I have been obsessed with Japanese fashion ever since I was a teenager and bought my first copy of Harajuku style bible *Fruits* magazine. Flipping through those pages I had never seen anything quite like it, the layering, the bright colours and the cute kawaii vibes. My style has evolved since then and my Japanese influence is maybe more subtle now with a nod to the kimono in one piece or the traditional geta shoe in another. Luckily Japanese fashion influences many of my favourite Melbourne designers as I believe there to be a huge following of Japanese food and design in Melbourne, the city is seemingly just as obsessed as I am with new late night izakayas popping up and a number of Harajuku-style crepe houses as well as Australia's first Comme Des Garçons store.

On Melburnian style

Melbourne people love to support Melbourne designers, and they love to interpret the clothes in their own way, but there's still elements that everyone will have ... It's kind of hard to explain. I guess I would describe the Melbourne fashionista as very inner-city. She rides a bicycle, she is interested in fair trade and ethical fashion, and she's politically minded. But she's very creative and just loves to dress up and express herself through fashion.

On what keeps her in Melbourne
Melbourne to me is home. It's where my friends and family are (well most of them anyway) and it's where I grew up. I have, of course, lived in Tokyo for one year and Sydney for three years – but like that old saying, there's no place like home.

For me Melbourne is simply the best city in Australia, which I know can be a controversial statement to make around people from other Australian cities, which I understand, as every city has its charm. However for me, after living in Sydney for three years and visiting all the other capital cities of Australia for work, Melbourne just has the most creative vibe of anywhere in Australia. There's always something happening, whether it's an art festival, a new boutique opening or even a food truck festival – so it's never boring.

What I love most about Melbourne though is the street style. Melbournites dress in a creative and expressive way, mixing vintage with designer brands in a way that is less about status and more about creating your own unique style. I'm always inspired just by looking around me, getting on the tram is it's own little fashion show and I love that.

Knot

Her speckled bleached jeans were what caught my eye first, but then she turned around and the outfit was brought to a whole other level.

Rough layers

NOTES

The yellow hair, the yellow skirt, the yellow bananas!

Jersey girl

Tokyo

Little bear

Twin set

The attitude she walked with ... This woman basically owned the Shibuya crossroads.

Ros Lee in Tokyo

I first discovered Ros Lee on Instagram, having stumbled upon her handmade pots and textile goods. Originally from Singapore, she has called Japan home for the last ten years. Her quirky and cute approach to her work is also reflected in her street style, which has a bit of a tomboy edge.

On her personal style

Growing up I was surrounded with craft supplies, because my family actually ran a craft supply business. I was very exposed to different materials and colours and that kind of inspired my creativity.

I remember my first ambition was to be a fashion designer. So I was, like, eight, but I loved looking at clothes and drawing. I liked matching up colourful pieces and patterns and stuff like that. So that was my style when I was young, very inspired by '80s fashion. And as a teenager, I was into grunge music, so I was wearing jeans and became a bit of a tomboy with my thick glasses and bangs.

But now, I guess my style has become a bit more reserved, rather than alternative. I toned it down when I was working an office job, so it was a bit more acceptable, but now that I'm working for myself I've started bringing in a bit more colours and I'm having fun with it again. I guess I've found that balance between the alternative and conservative.

On her fashion influences

I think music has always played a big influence on my style. I had a little band with my sister growing up, I was a bassist and we would play gigs and silly stuff like that. I always looked to different musicians and genres and would have fun with experimenting.

I also look to the past a lot for inspiration. Especially here in Japan. Oh, one thing I'd like to pick up, which is quite obviously traditionally Japanese, would be kimono. Like, I started learning just a few sessions of how to wear the kimono because I love the modern prints on kimono and stuff like that, but the after the session I realised, 'Oh, I can't really commit to this long-term study of how to wear the kimono', because there's, like, an endless number of strings that you need to tie before, and then a towel, and then another layer, and then another layer before you can even put it on, so I just didn't have the capacity to memorise all the steps. But I hope one day I can wear a kimono, you know, casually, like going out with friends and just as my daily wear. That would be awesome if I can ever, you know, remember the steps. Yeah, it's tough.

On Edokko style

Japan overall is very big on trends. So, when I moved here ten years ago, girls were very much into the 'girly' look. Harajuku style was obviously very big, but when it came to the mainstream, it was more about having light brown hair and wearing platforms heels, short skirts and being very feminine and attractive to the guys. Now, it's the complete opposite, the boyish look is in. Everyone is in button up tops with a sweater and sneakers.

Japanese people look to very famous people or influential models to know what to wear and what's cool. It's been like the last 20–30 years and with Instagram and everything online it's even easier to be on top of things and grab onto the trends. It's cool to be trendy which is probably different to many other places around the world.

On what keeps her in Tokyo

One of the things I really love about being here are the traditional crafts, like, old toys, you know the kokeshi dolls and things like that. And now there's a little revival going on and people are making things by hand and there are so many markets and events to go to and discover new things. Handmade is regarded as a really good craft and people treasure it, even in food. Like, if I visit a friend, and they make really nice home-cooked food, and they put so much detail into the presentation. It's the little things that I really appreciate. The attention to detail and the aesthetics part of Japan is what I love most about it.

NOTES

The difference a decade makes in trends: the 'girly' Harajuku uniform is slowly being replaced by more utilitarian, oversized, androgynous looks.

Village denim

NOTES

The fun, colourful, cheerful Tokyo street style is still going strong, with an even more high-fashion bent than in the past.

Kawaii

TOWN

Madrid

ESPECIALES
TARJETONES

Beatnik

NOTES

The kaleidoscopic effect of patterns and colours on the streets of Madrid is evident. A mix of classic and contemporary.

Black crop

Leyre Valiente in Madrid

Originally from a small town outside Madrid, Leyre Valiente's imagination has always been out of this world. Citing the '70s film *Alien* as a source of inspiration in her personal style and work as a fashion designer, Leyre's fantastic creations wouldn't look out of place being worn by the likes of Lady Gaga.

On her personal style

I had a little bit of bullying during high school, because I was a nerd. I studied a lot and I liked weird things like manga and just alternative culture. But I was happy. I have always been a happy person.

I remember watching *Labyrinth* with David Bowie and the next day I went to school, like, imitating the look of Jennifer Connelly in the movie, or things like that, or maybe inspired by manga aesthetics, by Japanese aesthetics, so, yeah, I had a period very inspired by manga.

Headbands with big ribbons, Japanese big ribbons, and the different kind of glasses, like, lots of brooches. I had a time when I used to make hand brooches and I used to wear, like, three for example. A guy once told me that I was like colourful gothic, yeah, and a girl told me it was creepy but cute.

But I also wanted to be Punky Brewster, I wanted to be Blossom. I used to wear lots of hats, all kinds of hats with a flower here, with all kinds of hats. I went to school with hats, and people in school didn't understand it.

It's those things that got me thinking about fashion and the aesthetics of my own style. As an adult now, it's been a bit more refined.

On her fashion influences

Well, when I was a kid I loved the movie, *Working Girl*, with Melanie Griffith and Sigourney Weaver. I love them with the high heels and with the big shoulders and with the big attitude, the big hair. When people asked me what I wanted to be when I grew up, instead of saying ballerina or whatever, I said: 'I want to be an aggressive businesswoman.' I didn't know what it meant, I just wanted to wear high heels and enter the building with that attitude and lots of men serving you. Maybe because I was bullied by boys, I wanted that respect they had, that strength – I think that's where my inspiration for my designs come from, they're influenced by big strong women, I tend to focus my attention in the big shoulders, maybe because of that movie.

On Madrileño style

In Spain we had the Franco dictatorship and we couldn't express ourselves a lot, there wasn't much of a culture for many years in my opinion. So when it came to fashion we are a little behind, but now the young people are working on it, trying to experiment with new stuff, with new kinds of style.

I think we were stuck in the sexy Latino thing but we're now evolving and leaving that behind. Maybe a bit more European now, the mixing of genders, in an open-minded way. I am a teacher too, so I work with fashion students and I can see that every day. Some students are working way ahead of what we used to do in Spain, which is really great.

On what keeps her in Madrid

In this very moment I see it in my classes in the schools. I see, like, a lot of new thinking, a lot of new things, a lot of hunger for doing new things, working hard get to do great things, and we have that strength now, and I want to be a part of that. You can see the things we did and the things we're doing now and how we are working, and if you see lots of new designers, you're going to see that they are doing great things. We don't have that name internationally because we haven't been that big a country in fashion or design, but we are doing great things, and I think we are going to change things, and maybe in ten years or twenty years, a lot of people are going to be very, very important. There are already designers rocking it in New York, and they are Spanish. We are getting there.

Calvins

Classic floral

From the brogues to the blazer; variations on this menswear-inspired style represent the most pervasive look I observed around the world in the past year.

Flat top

NOTES

Modern cuts and colour blocking; not typical of the Spanish woman but a growing movement.

TIME TO
DRINK
CHAMPAGNE
AND DANCE
Vacations
ON THE
TABLE

Short shorts

Bomber

TOWN

London

Jump

Button up

NOTES

The layers were magical; from the colours, the patterns and the textures. More is always more.

Chelsea Bravo in London

Hailing from North London, Chelsea Bravo is an up-and-coming fashion designer, taking on the world of menswear. She beautifully exemplifies the current generation of young women who are doing things their own way, unfazed by the rules of the fashion world.

On her personal style

I'm pretty comfortable with my style and I feel like it will probably stay this way for a while. I love oversized. I love kind of a tomboy feel to what I wear – but still feel feminine with jewellery, I have loads of dangly sort of silver earrings. I just like to be comfortable. I feel like I've started playing around more with my style.

When I was younger, there was this TV show called *Clueless*, which I was addicted to. I remember one night I was staying up with my dad and we watched the movie together, and I was just, like, mesmerised by these girls. I thought they were everything. I didn't have a lot of things that looked like what they wore – but I remember having this one skirt, that was kind of like a tartan-type skirt, because they wore a lot of these pleated, sort of tartan skirts. So I had that one skirt, I had some cream, knee-high socks, some black little loafer shoes with little heels. I thought: 'Yeah, perfect, this is Cher.'

On her fashion influences

My mum would buy fashion magazines all the time when I was younger and I would look through those a lot, so I think she helped influence my interest in fashion growing up.

Now that I'm designing menswear, I've very much discovered this whole new world of [fashion], specifically the Japanese aesthetic. I think you can see it in my designs and even the way I dress.

On Londoner style

Right now, there is a massive masculine influence and I think we're just feeling more empowered, very strong-willed. We know what we want. We're not relying on, you know, men to kind of, like, lead the way or kind of, like, provide for us.

Not too long ago, it was all about the bodycon. You know, the bandage dresses that every girl was wearing? So everything was kind of, like, this fitted type of thing. I think it's more interesting to leave something to the imagination, a little bit of curiosity, don't give everything away – it's so much more intriguing that way.

I definitely think that this is shining through on the high street. You know brands like Celine, they have a massive influence on what the high street put out on the shop floor and I feel like it's this almost sort of feminine masculinity.

Selfridges right now, they have the Agender project, and they're exploring and talking about this topic called genderless shopping and I think the slogan they have is 'He, She, Me'. It's basically just saying, why does it have to kind of be male/female. Why can't I just decide what I want to wear, you know, and let it be that?

On what keeps her in London
The food. You've got Indian, Chinese, Mexican and good-old English foods all in a block's radius. That's one of the great things about London. The South Bank is such a lovely place to go to in the summer, they have amazing restaurants down there – such a great atmosphere.

Also, the fact that you meet such a different range of people by living here. I have friends who are from Korea, Paris, India and Canada who I've met in the last few years. So many people from different walks of life and from different countries, I think that's important to surround yourself with. I'm very much interested in people from different cultures to myself. I learn more about life and see that there isn't just one way of going about it. I love London for that.

It's also very accessible, I mean, you can travel very easily here. I've been to Paris and I've been to New York and I hope to do a lot more travelling in the future.

Spotted on Oxford Street, the trench has become a London icon. Quite like the beret in Paris.

Wings

Top knot

Cross

NOTES

What is there to say? She's just lovely.

Quilt

Wild

ABOUT THE AUTHOR

Giuseppe Santamaria is a photographer and editor, originally from Toronto, Canada. He moved to Sydney, Australia, nine years ago and lives there with his partner, Josh and their Boston terrier, Baxter.

Follow his work at *womeninthistown.com* and *meninthistown.com*, and his life through pictures on Instagram @giuseppeinthistown.

Men in this Town: London, Tokyo, Sydney, Milan, New York

From five distinct cities around the world – London, Tokyo, Sydney, Milan and New York – photographer Giuseppe Santamaria brings together a unique photographic collection showcasing the street styles of the modern man. Alongside striking images captured from the streets, Giuseppe has profiled a handful of men from each city about their particular approach to fashion and their sense of the menswear scene today. *Men in this Town* will fascinate anyone with an interest in fashion, photography, and the street-style culture of the everyday man across the world.

MITT magazine

Based on the men's street style blog *Men in this Town*, *MITT* is a printed quarterly digest capturing the everyday man in his natural habitat. Through profiles, interviews, features and photo essays, *MITT* takes a closer look at who the men on the street are and their particular approach to the many facets of life.

ACKNOWLEDGEMENTS

Thank you Josh for your never-ending support.
You push me to better myself and my work in
more ways than you know.

To my loving family, thank you for being my
biggest fans, even if you don't exactly know what
I do. Thank you Dom.

To Hardie Grant for believing in a second book
and bringing my online projects to life in the
printed form.

Thank you to the women profiled in this book,
your words and your lives are inspiring and I
hope they speak to the younger women who pick
up this book.

Thank you to Olympus Australia for supporting
me on this journey around the world, capturing
the moments with my OM-D EM5II.

And lastly Baxter, thank you for taking care of
big dog while I was away from home.

Published in 2015 by Hardie Grant Books

Hardie Grant Books (Australia)
Ground Floor, Building 1
658 Church Street
Richmond, Victoria 3121
www.hardiegrant.com.au

Hardie Grant Books (UK)
5th & 6th Floors
52–54 Southwark Street
London SE1 1UN
www.hardiegrant.co.uk

A Cataloguing-in-Publication entry is available from the catalogue
of the National Library of Australia at www.nla.gov.au
Women in this Town
9781743790205

Publishing Director: Paul McNally
Project Editor: Hannah Koelmeyer
Design Manager: Mark Campbell
Designer: Giuseppe Santamaria
Production Manager: Todd Rechner

Colour reproduction by Splitting Image Colour Studio
Printed and bound in China by 1010 Printing International Limited